JULIA ROTHMAN

FARM

FOOD

NATURE

Engagement Calendar 2021

WORKMAN PUBLISHING • NEW YORK

WORKMAN and PAGE-A-DAY are registered
trademarks of Workman Publishing Co., Inc.

Design by Gordon Whiteside

Workman calendars and diaries are available
at special discounts when purchased in bulk for
premiums and sales promotions as well as for fund-
raising or educational use. Special editions can also
be created to specification. For details, contact the
Special Sales Director at the address below, or send
an email to specialmarkets@workman.com.

ISBN 978-1-5235-1128-0

Printed in South Korea
Printed on FSC®-certified paper

Workman Publishing Co., Inc.
225 Varick Street
New York, NY 10014-4381

pageaday.com

This calendar contains material that was
previously published in the books *Farm Anatomy*,
Food Anatomy, and *Nature Anatomy*
by Julia Rothman.

This book belongs to

Welcome to your
Farm, Food, Nature
2021 Engagement Calendar

Farm, Food, and Nature. As I've worked on the book series through the years, I've realized how interconnected these subjects are: Through farming, we harness nature's resources to produce food that sustains our lives and allows us, in turn, to express ourselves and our cultures throughout the world. And though I've been drawn to the outdoors ever since I was young, I grew up in a big city, so the idea of living in a rural area seemed so foreign to me. I have a great appreciation for the natural world that peeks through in my city of New York, undaunted by the skyscrapers surrounding it—you'd be surprised by how many ingredients for a colorful salad are living in your local park—and having spent a good amount of time on farms, I am always amazed by how comparably lush, expansive, and full of curiosities they are.

In these pages, you'll find drawings and step-by-step sequences that reveal everything from the wide variety of bird beaks to how an orchard gets planted to the anatomy of a food truck. As the year passes with each week's plans and to-dos, embark on a visual tour of life on the farm, the culinary world, and the Earth that we all inhabit. In a modern world that's always encouraging us to speed to the next thing, taking a moment to resituate yourself in the natural side of life can create stability, an anchor to the earth and its bounty that we reap.

I hope that this planner will inspire you to go on more food adventures, gain an appreciation for the ideals of country life, and be curious about your own backyard, whether it's acres of wheat or a flower box on a fire escape.

Julia
Rothman

COMMON BARN STYLES

Gable

Gambrel

Monitor

Gothic

28
MONDAY

29
TUESDAY

FULL MOON ○

30
WEDNESDAY

31
THURSDAY

1
FRIDAY

NEW YEAR'S DAY

2
SATURDAY

3
SUNDAY

		JANUARY				
S	M	T	W	T	F	S
					1	2
3	4	5	6	7	8	9
10	11	12	13	14	15	16
17	18	19	20	21	22	23
24	25	26	27	28	29	30
31						

Notes

A SPOT OF TEA

Real tea — everything else is just an herbal infusion — is made from the leaves and leaf buds of just one Asian shrub: *Camellia sinensis*. Though there are many cultivars and special growing regions, all tea is harvested from just two main varieties: Chinese and Indian Assam.

CAMELLIA SINENSIS

white or yellow

tender new shoots, picked only a few days per year, then quickly dried to avoid any oxidation

green

tea leaves that are quickly dried after harvest to avoid any oxidation

oolong

large, mature leaves allowed to oxidize slightly before they're dried

black

younger tea leaves that are bruised and fully oxidized before being dried

pu-erh

tea leaves that are allowed to ferment and age

January 2021

4
MONDAY   BANK HOLIDAY (SCOTLAND & NEW ZEALAND)

5
TUESDAY

LAST QUARTER ◑

6
WEDNESDAY

7
THURSDAY

8
FRIDAY

9
SATURDAY

10
SUNDAY

JANUARY

S	M	T	W	T	F	S
					1	2
3	4	5	6	7	8	9
10	11	12	13	14	15	16
17	18	19	20	21	22	23
24	25	26	27	28	29	30
31						

Notes

How a Flower Becomes a Fruit

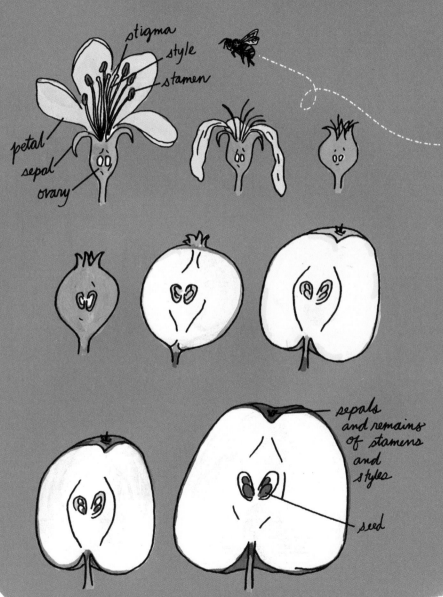

11
MONDAY

12
TUESDAY

NEW MOON ●

13
WEDNESDAY

14
THURSDAY

15
FRIDAY

MARTIN LUTHER KING JR.'S BIRTHDAY

16
SATURDAY

17
SUNDAY

JANUARY

S	M	T	W	T	F	S
					1	2
3	4	5	6	7	8	9
10	11	12	13	14	15	16
17	18	19	20	21	22	23
24	25	26	27	28	29	30
31						

Notes

ANATOMY OF A DECIDUOUS TREE

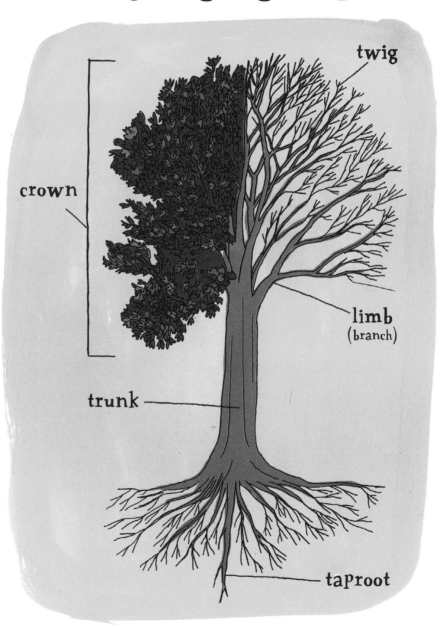

twig

crown

limb
(branch)

trunk

taproot

18
MONDAY

MARTIN LUTHER KING JR. DAY

19
TUESDAY

FIRST QUARTER ◐

20
WEDNESDAY

21
THURSDAY

22
FRIDAY

23
SATURDAY

24
SUNDAY

JANUARY

S	M	T	W	T	F	S
					1	2
3	4	5	6	7	8	9
10	11	12	13	14	15	16
17	18	19	20	21	22	23
24	25	26	27	28	29	30
31						

Notes

Black Bear

- weighs between 100 and 600 pounds
- upright ears
- flat shoulder
- rump higher than shoulder
- rounded (convex) profile

VS.

Grizzly Bear

- weighs between 300 and 800 pounds
- rounder, shorter ears
- shoulder hump
- sloping rump
- dished (concave) profile

January 2021

25
MONDAY

26
TUESDAY

AUSTRALIA DAY (AUSTRALIA)

27
WEDNESDAY

FULL MOON ○

28
THURSDAY

29
FRIDAY

30
SATURDAY

31
SUNDAY

JANUARY

S	M	T	W	T	F	S
					1	2
3	4	5	6	7	8	9
10	11	12	13	14	15	16
17	18	19	20	21	22	23
24	25	26	27	28	29	30
31						

Notes

PIZZA, PIZZA!

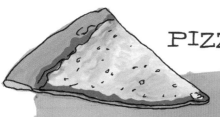

New York Slice

Sold at small pizza places on every street, this plain cheese slice usually costs little more than a dollar or two.

Sicilian Pizza Slice

In America, this is a thick square pie with a crunchy base and generally a fluffy, airy, almost bready crust.

New Jersey Tomato Pie

A thick, dense crust is topped with a thick layer of crushed tomatoes and a small amount of grated cheese, similar in style to the *sfincione* made in the Sicilian city of Palermo.

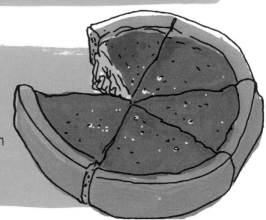

Chicago Deep Dish

Pizza cooked in a deep-sided pie pan; the cheese generally goes underneath the toppings with the sauce on top.

Pizza al Taglio

This Roman-style pizza is baked in long rectangular pans in electric ovens and often cut with scissors and sold by weight.

Detroit Deep Dish

A thick, chewy crusted pizza related to the Sicilian, baked in a well-oiled pan so that the crust appears almost fried; it is sometimes baked twice.

Neapolitan Pizza Margherita

Originating near the Italian city of Naples, with a puffy crust made possible in part by quick cooking in a wood-fired oven, this pizza should be made with basil, tomatoes from San Marzano, and buffalo milk mozzarella from Campania.

St. Louis Pizza

It has cracker-thin crust topped with Provel (a white processed-cheese blend of cheddar, Swiss, and provolone) and is cut into squares.

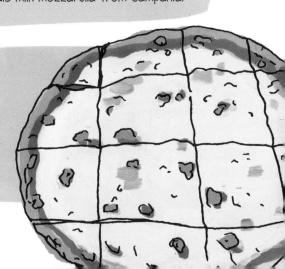

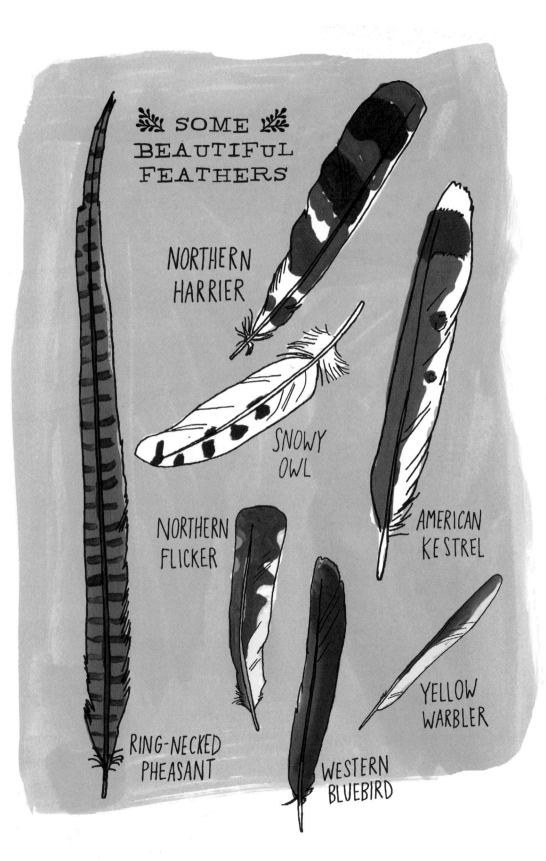

1
MONDAY

2
TUESDAY

3
WEDNESDAY

LAST QUARTER ◑

4
THURSDAY

5
FRIDAY

6
SATURDAY

WAITANGI DAY (NEW ZEALAND)

7
SUNDAY

FEBRUARY

S	M	T	W	T	F	S
	1	2	3	4	5	6
7	8	9	10	11	12	13
14	15	16	17	18	19	20
21	22	23	24	25	26	27
28						

Notes

KINDS OF SPOONS

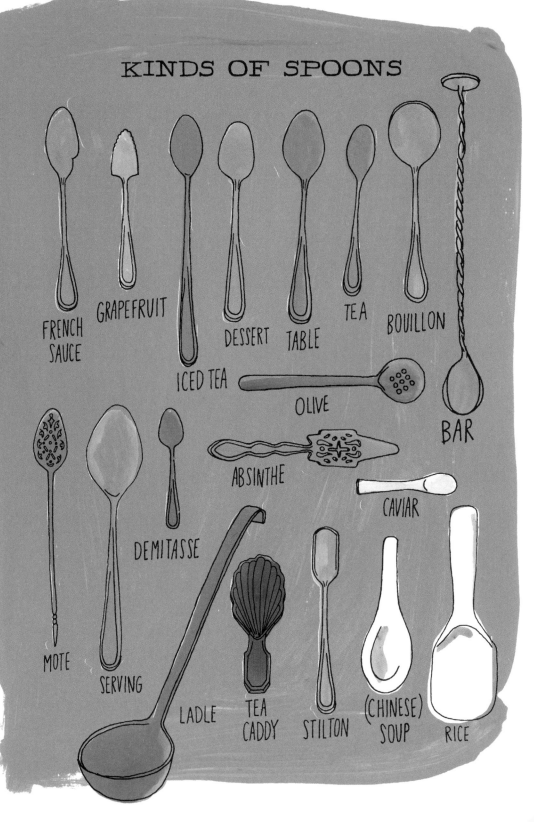

FRENCH SAUCE

GRAPEFRUIT

ICED TEA

DESSERT

TABLE

TEA

BOUILLON

OLIVE

BAR

MOTE

DEMITASSE

ABSINTHE

CAVIAR

SERVING

LADLE

TEA CADDY

STILTON

(CHINESE) SOUP

RICE

8
MONDAY

9
TUESDAY

10
WEDNESDAY

NEW MOON ●

11
THURSDAY

12
FRIDAY

LUNAR NEW YEAR • LINCOLN'S BIRTHDAY

13
SATURDAY

14
SUNDAY

VALENTINE'S DAY

FEBRUARY

S	M	T	W	T	F	S
	1	2	3	4	5	6
7	8	9	10	11	12	13
14	15	16	17	18	19	20
21	22	23	24	25	26	27
28						

Notes

The Water Cycle

Precipitation

Condensation
releases energy and
warms the environment

Evaporation
takes energy and
cools the environment

Surface
runoff

Water is the only substance
on Earth to naturally appear
as liquid, solid, and vapor.

In the natural world, water is always moving and changing its form.
It travels from streams to rivers to oceans, from lakes and oceans
to the atmosphere, and from the atmosphere back to land. This cycle
slowly purifies water and replenishes the land with fresh water.

15
MONDAY

PRESIDENTS DAY • FAMILY DAY (CANADA)

16
TUESDAY

17
WEDNESDAY

ASH WEDNESDAY

18
THURSDAY

FIRST QUARTER ◑

19
FRIDAY

20
SATURDAY

21
SUNDAY

FEBRUARY						
S	M	T	W	T	F	S
	1	2	3	4	5	6
7	8	9	10	11	12	13
14	15	16	17	18	19	20
21	22	23	24	25	26	27
28						

Notes

PARTS OF A ROOSTER

1. comb
2. earlobe
3. cape
4. saddle
5. sickles
6. fluff
7. thigh
8. hock
9. spur
10. claw
11. shank
12. breast
13. hackles
14. wattles
15. beak

22
MONDAY

WASHINGTON'S BIRTHDAY

23
TUESDAY

24
WEDNESDAY

25
THURSDAY

26
FRIDAY

FULL MOON ○

27
SATURDAY

28
SUNDAY

FEBRUARY

S	M	T	W	T	F	S
	1	2	3	4	5	6
7	8	9	10	11	12	13
14	15	16	17	18	19	20
21	22	23	24	25	26	27
28						

Notes

AN ACRE IS...

43,560 square feet

4,840 square yards

1/640 square mile

0.4047 hectare

160 perches

4 roods

A SECTION IS...

1 square mile

640 acres

1
MONDAY   LABOUR DAY (WA AUSTRALIA)

2
TUESDAY

3
WEDNESDAY

4
THURSDAY

5
FRIDAY

                                                      LAST QUARTER ◑

6
SATURDAY

7
SUNDAY

MARCH

S	M	T	W	T	F	S
	1	2	3	4	5	6
7	8	9	10	11	12	13
14	15	16	17	18	19	20
21	22	23	24	25	26	27
28	29	30	31			

Notes

Cut the Cheese

A great cheese plate displays a range of flavors, textures, shapes, and colors. Use cheeses made from different types of milk, of different ages, all cut into different shapes. It also demands accompaniments, usually sweet ones: Try a few types of excellent honey, fig or other fruit preserves, or a selection of dried fruits and nuts.

Cut along dotted line.

WEDGE

SEMISOFT WEDGE

VEINED WEDGE

WHEEL

LOG

PYRAMID

CHEESE KNIVES

SOFT CHEESE

SERVING FORK

HARD CHEESE

BLUE CHEESE

CHEESE PLANE

TRADITIONAL

8
MONDAY

LABOUR DAY (VIC AUSTRALIA)

9
TUESDAY

10
WEDNESDAY

LAILAT AL-MIRAJ BEGINS AT SUNDOWN

11
THURSDAY

12
FRIDAY

NEW MOON ●

13
SATURDAY

14
SUNDAY

DAYLIGHT SAVING TIME BEGINS AT 2:00 A.M. (US & CANADA)

MARCH						
S	M	T	W	T	F	S
	1	2	3	4	5	6
7	8	9	10	11	12	13
14	15	16	17	18	19	20
21	22	23	24	25	26	27
28	29	30	31			

Notes

A Variety of Beaks

WHITE - THROATED
SPARROW

great for crushing seeds
and pecking at bark
to uncover hiding insects

RINGED
KINGFISHER

wedge shape creates
no splash when entering
the water

MALLARD
DUCK

used for skimming
in shallow waters

BALD EAGLE

hooked for tearing up prey

RED
CROSSBILL

helps with prying
apart scales of a
pinecone

RUBY-THROATED
HUMMINGBIRD

long, to probe
into flowers

SPOONBILL

partly open bill sweeps
through water to find
prey, then snaps shut
to capture it

15
MONDAY

16
TUESDAY

17
WEDNESDAY

ST. PATRICK'S DAY

18
THURSDAY

19
FRIDAY

20
SATURDAY

FIRST QUARTER ◗

21
SUNDAY

MARCH

S	M	T	W	T	F	S
		1	2	3	4	5	6
7	8	9	10	11	12	13
14	15	16	17	18	19	20
21	22	23	24	25	26	27
28	29	30	31			

Notes

ANATOMY OF A BEE

1. **antenna** - contains thousands of tiny sensors that detect smell
2. **compound eye** - for general distance sight
3. **ocellus** - three simple eyes used for low light conditions in the hive
4. **thorax** - segment between head and abdomen where wings attach
5. **forewing**
6. **hindwing** ⎤ — 2-part wings hook together in flight but separate at rest
7. **abdomen** - contains all the organs, wax glands, and stinger
8. **stinger** - only present on worker and queen bees
9. **femur**
10. **tibia** ⎤ — three pairs of legs with six segments each;
11. **tarsal claw** ⎦ used for walking and packing pollen

22
MONDAY

23
TUESDAY

24
WEDNESDAY

25
THURSDAY

26
FRIDAY

27
SATURDAY

PASSOVER BEGINS AT SUNDOWN

FULL MOON ○

28
SUNDAY

PALM SUNDAY

MARCH						
S	M	T	W	T	F	S
	1	2	3	4	5	6
7	8	9	10	11	12	13
14	15	16	17	18	19	20
21	22	23	24	25	26	27
28	29	30	31			

Notes

ON AVERAGE

1
HEN

LAYS

260 EGGS PER YEAR

29
MONDAY

30
TUESDAY

31
WEDNESDAY

1
THURSDAY

2
FRIDAY

GOOD FRIDAY

3
SATURDAY

LAST QUARTER ◑

4
SUNDAY

EASTER

APRIL

S	M	T	W	T	F	S
				1	2	3
4	5	6	7	8	9	10
11	12	13	14	15	16	17
18	19	20	21	22	23	24
25	26	27	28	29	30	

Notes..

SHORT ORDER EGG LINGO

ADAM + EVE
ON A LOG

ADAM + EVE
ON A RAFT

ADAM + EVE
ON A RAFT
AND WRECK 'EM

CLUCK + GRUNT

COWBOY
WESTERN

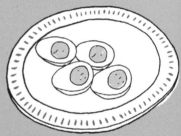

DROWN THE KIDS
(boil the eggs)

ETERNAL TWINS

FRY TWO
LET THE
SUN SHINE

FAMILY
REUNION

KISS THE PAN

MAKE IT
CRACKLE

SCRAPE TWO

TWO DOTS +
A DASH

WRECKED
+ CRYING

WRECKED
HEN WITH
FRUIT

DOUGH WELL
DONE WITH
COW TO COVER

SHINGLE WITH
A SHIMMY
+ A SHAKE

BURN THE
BRITISH

AVERAGE DATES OF LAST SPRING FROST

It's safe to plant most crops after the last frost of the spring.

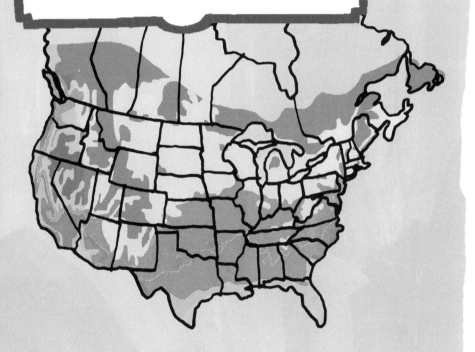

- JUNE 1 – JULY 31
- MAY 1 – MAY 31
- APRIL 1 – APRIL 30
- MARCH 1 – MARCH 31
- FEBRUARY 1 – FEBRUARY 28
- JANUARY 1 – JANUARY 31

5
MONDAY

EASTER MONDAY BANK HOLIDAY (ENG., WALES, N. IRE., AUSTRAL., NZ)

6
TUESDAY

7
WEDNESDAY

8
THURSDAY

9
FRIDAY

10
SATURDAY

11
SUNDAY

APRIL

S	M	T	W	T	F	S
				1	2	3
4	5	6	7	8	9	10
11	12	13	14	15	16	17
18	19	20	21	22	23	24
25	26	27	28	29	30	

Notes

A SPOONFUL OF SUGAR

In the United States, dark brown or light brown sugar is most commonly made from refined white sugar crystals with added molasses.

Demerara, turbinado, and muscovado sugars — sometimes called "raw" sugars — are made by retaining some of the molasses naturally found in sugarcane as the sugar is processed. These vary in crystal size and intensity of flavor.

The most deeply flavored sugars come from evaporated, unprocessed sugarcane juice, rich with molasses. Depending on the country, this is called panela, rapadura, jaggery, piloncillo, kokuto — all of which come in dense blocks, rather than crystals — or unrefined whole cane sugar.

White

Brown

Light Brown

Turbinado

Muscovado

Unrefined Whole Cane Sugar

NEW MOON ●

12
MONDAY

RAMADAN BEGINS AT SUNDOWN

13
TUESDAY

14
WEDNESDAY

15
THURSDAY

16
FRIDAY

17
SATURDAY

18
SUNDAY

APRIL						
S	M	T	W	T	F	S
				1	2	3
4	5	6	7	8	9	10
11	12	13	14	15	16	17
18	19	20	21	22	23	24
25	26	27	28	29	30	

Notes

ANATOMY OF A MUSHROOM

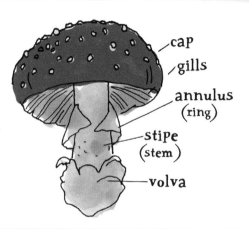

- cap
- gills
- annulus (ring)
- stipe (stem)
- volva

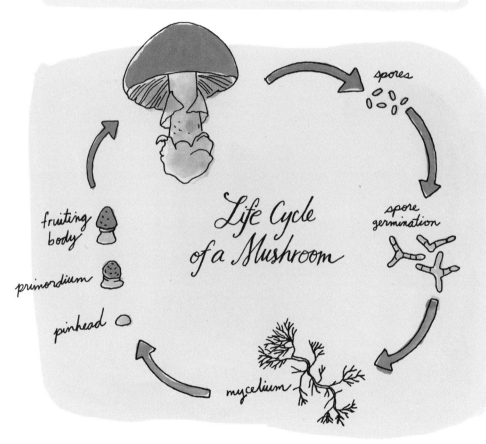

Life Cycle of a Mushroom

- spores
- spore germination
- mycelium
- pinhead
- primordium
- fruiting body

19
MONDAY

FIRST QUARTER ◑

20
TUESDAY

21
WEDNESDAY

22
THURSDAY

EARTH DAY

23
FRIDAY

24
SATURDAY

25
SUNDAY

ANZAC DAY (AUSTRALIA & NEW ZEALAND)

APRIL						
S	M	T	W	T	F	S
				1	2	3
4	5	6	7	8	9	10
11	12	13	14	15	16	17
18	19	20	21	22	23	24
25	26	27	28	29	30	

Notes

PARTS OF A HORSE

1. muzzle
2. forelock
3. poll
4. crest
5. withers
6. loin
7. hip
8. croup
9. dock
10. point of buttocks
11. hock
12. gaskin
13. flank
14. barrel
15. fetlock
16. hoof
17. coronet
18. pastern
19. cannon
20. forearm
21. shoulder
22. throatlatch
23. cheek

26
MONDAY

FULL MOON ○

27
TUESDAY

28
WEDNESDAY

29
THURSDAY

30
FRIDAY

1
SATURDAY

2
SUNDAY

ORTHODOX EASTER

MAY

S	M	T	W	T	F	S
						1
2	3	4	5	6	7	8
9	10	11	12	13	14	15
16	17	18	19	20	21	22
23	24	25	26	27	28	29
30	31					

Notes

Planting an Orchard

When planting an orchard, you need to consider that many trees require cross-pollination. That means you need to plant at least two varieties of each type of fruit tree. Mostly the trees are pollinated by bees, so planning the distance between the trees is important. The two kinds shouldn't be more than 500 feet from each other.

CROSS-POLLINATION

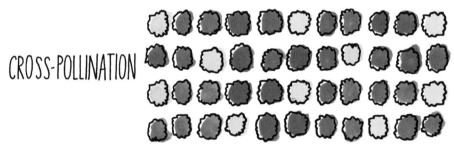

In large orchards, pollenizer trees are scattered among the others.

Dwarf fruit trees produce fruit the same size and flavor as standard trees, but are easier to maintain and harvest.

LAST QUARTER ◑

3
MONDAY

BANK HOLIDAY (UNITED KINGDOM) • LABOUR DAY (QLD AUSTRALIA)

4
TUESDAY

5
WEDNESDAY

6
THURSDAY

7
FRIDAY

8
SATURDAY

9
SUNDAY

MOTHER'S DAY

MAY

S	M	T	W	T	F	S
						1
2	3	4	5	6	7	8
9	10	11	12	13	14	15
16	17	18	19	20	21	22
23	24	25	26	27	28	29
30	31					

Notes

❦ A BEVY OF BIRDS ❦

Flocks have been known to line up on a branch and pass berries down the line beak to beak until every bird has been fed.

CEDAR WAXWING

FLORIDA SCRUB JAY

Scrub jays have cooperative families in which fledglings stay with their parents, helping feed and tend to subsequent hatchlings.

WHITE-BREASTED NUTHATCH

This is one of the only birds to descend trees headfirst.

SCISSOR-TAILED FLYCATCHER

The male performs a number of acrobatic mid-air somersaults in its courtship display.

BELTED KINGFISHER

It gives a loud clattering call before diving headfirst into lakes or rivers to snatch fish.

10
MONDAY

NEW MOON ●

11
TUESDAY

12
WEDNESDAY

EID AL-FITR BEGINS AT SUNDOWN

13
THURSDAY

14
FRIDAY

15
SATURDAY

16
SUNDAY

		MAY				
S	M	T	W	T	F	S
						1
2	3	4	5	6	7	8
9	10	11	12	13	14	15
16	17	18	19	20	21	22
23	24	25	26	27	28	29
30	31					

Notes

BEANS

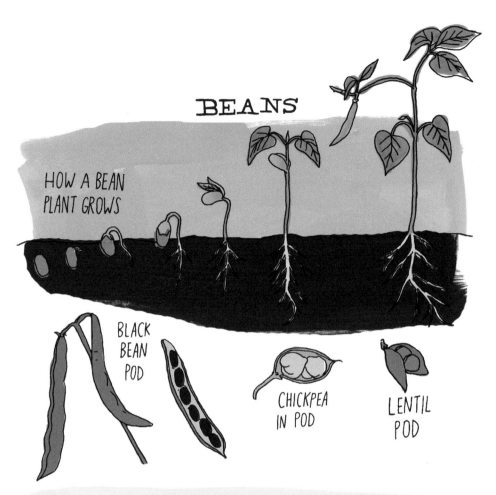

HOW A BEAN PLANT GROWS

BLACK BEAN POD

CHICKPEA IN POD

LENTIL POD

Bean Varieties

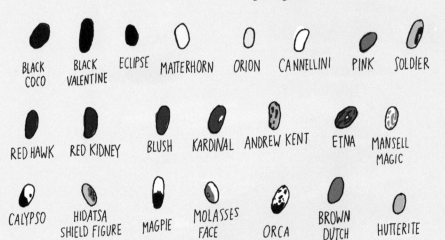

BLACK COCO · BLACK VALENTINE · ECLIPSE · MATTERHORN · ORION · CANNELLINI · PINK · SOLDIER

RED HAWK · RED KIDNEY · BLUSH · KARDINAL · ANDREW KENT · ETNA · MANSELL MAGIC

CALYPSO · HIDATSA SHIELD FIGURE · MAGPIE · MOLASSES FACE · ORCA · BROWN DUTCH · HUTTERITE

17
MONDAY

18
TUESDAY

FIRST QUARTER ◗

19
WEDNESDAY

20
THURSDAY

21
FRIDAY

22
SATURDAY

23
SUNDAY

MAY						
S	M	T	W	T	F	S
						1
2	3	4	5	6	7	8
9	10	11	12	13	14	15
16	17	18	19	20	21	22
23	24	25	26	27	28	29
30	31					

Notes

ANATOMY OF A FOOD TRUCK

Based on plans from PrestigeFoodTrucks.com

24
MONDAY

VICTORIA DAY (CANADA)

25
TUESDAY

FULL MOON ○

26
WEDNESDAY

27
THURSDAY

28
FRIDAY

29
SATURDAY

30
SUNDAY

TRADITIONAL MEMORIAL DAY

MAY						
S	M	T	W	T	F	S
						1
2	3	4	5	6	7	8
9	10	11	12	13	14	15
16	17	18	19	20	21	22
23	24	25	26	27	28	29
30	31					

Notes

BUTTERFLY FAMILIES OF NORTH AMERICA

swallowtails (FAMILY PAPILIONIDAE)
medium to large, tail-like appendages on hindwings, colorful

brush-footed (FAMILY NYMPHALIDAE)
largest family, two shorter legs used for tasting food

whites + sulphurs (FAMILY PIERIDAE)
mostly white or yellow wings with black or orange marks

gossamer-winged (FAMILY LYCAENIDAE)
sheer wings, smaller sized, includes hairstreaks, blues and copper

metalmarks (FAMILY RIODINIDAE)
small to medium, mostly tropical, metallic marks

TRUE BUTTERFLIES

skippers (FAMILY HESPERIIDAE)
wide thoraxes, small wings, hooked antennae, brown and gray with white and orange marks

31
MONDAY

MEMORIAL DAY OBSERVED • SPRING BANK HOLIDAY (UNITED KINGDOM)

1
TUESDAY

LAST QUARTER ◗

2
WEDNESDAY

3
THURSDAY

4
FRIDAY

5
SATURDAY

6
SUNDAY

JUNE

S	M	T	W	T	F	S
		1	2	3	4	5
6	7	8	9	10	11	12
13	14	15	16	17	18	19
20	21	22	23	24	25	26
27	28	29	30			

Notes

Composting

Composting is the process that uses bacteria to decompose organic waste into nutrient-rich fertilizer. For best results, layers of nitrogen-rich (green) and carbon-rich (brown) ingredients are piled in a bin in a 3 to 1 ratio. Soil organisms break it down into nutritious organic matter in just over two weeks.

6"
2"

GREENS
high nitrogen

GARDEN WASTE
KITCHEN WASTE
GRASS CLIPPINGS
COFFEE GROUNDS
HAIR

BROWNS
high carbon

PAPER
DRY LEAVES
WOOD CHIPS
STRAW
SAWDUST

7
MONDAY QUEEN'S BIRTHDAY (NEW ZEALAND)

8
TUESDAY

9
WEDNESDAY

NEW MOON ●

10
THURSDAY

11
FRIDAY

12
SATURDAY

13
SUNDAY

JUNE

S	M	T	W	T	F	S
		1	2	3	4	5
6	7	8	9	10	11	12
13	14	15	16	17	18	19
20	21	22	23	24	25	26
27	28	29	30			

Notes

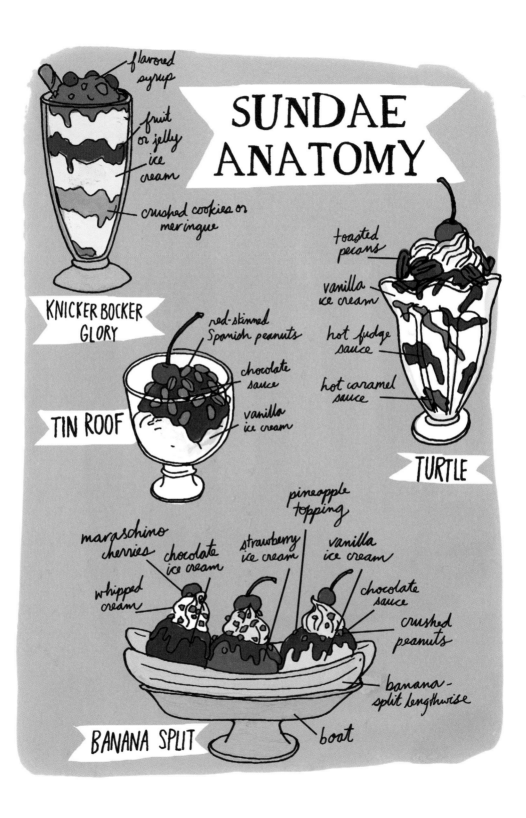

SUNDAE ANATOMY

KNICKER BOCKER GLORY
- flavored syrup
- fruit or jelly
- ice cream
- crushed cookies or meringue

TIN ROOF
- red-skinned Spanish peanuts
- chocolate sauce
- vanilla ice cream

TURTLE
- toasted pecans
- vanilla ice cream
- hot fudge sauce
- hot caramel sauce

BANANA SPLIT
- maraschino cherries
- chocolate ice cream
- whipped cream
- pineapple topping
- strawberry ice cream
- vanilla ice cream
- chocolate sauce
- crushed peanuts
- banana-split lengthwise
- boat

14
MONDAY

FLAG DAY • QUEEN'S BIRTHDAY (AUSTRALIA EXC. QLD & WA)

15
TUESDAY

16
WEDNESDAY

17
THURSDAY

FIRST QUARTER ◗

18
FRIDAY

19
SATURDAY

20
SUNDAY

FATHER'S DAY

JUNE						
S	M	T	W	T	F	S
		1	2	3	4	5
6	7	8	9	10	11	12
13	14	15	16	17	18	19
20	21	22	23	24	25	26
27	28	29	30			

Notes

EDIBLE PARTS OF FLOWERING PLANTS

Flower
BUTTER LEAF LETTUCE
Leaf
ARTICHOKE PLANT
SPINACH

Fruit
Seeds
PATTYPAN
SUNFLOWER SEEDS
TOMATO

Stem
ASPARAGUS (growing)
Root
HORSERADISH
CARROT

21
MONDAY

22
TUESDAY

23
WEDNESDAY

FULL MOON ○

24
THURSDAY

ST. JEAN BAPTISTE DAY (CANADA)

25
FRIDAY

26
SATURDAY

27
SUNDAY

JUNE						
S	M	T	W	T	F	S
		1	2	3	4	5
6	7	8	9	10	11	12
13	14	15	16	17	18	19
20	21	22	23	24	25	26
27	28	29	30			

Notes

American Pie

1. **BANANA CREAM** a custard pie made with sliced bananas and a graham cracker cookie crust, topped with whipped cream

2. **SOUR CHERRY** with a lattice crust

3. **LEMON MERINGUE** lemon curd filling topped with meringue (whipped egg whites and sugar)

4. **CHOCOLATE CHESS** Southern-style custard pie flavored with cocoa powder and thickened with cornmeal

5. **GRASSHOPPER** a mint-flavored, whipped cream-filled pie with a crushed chocolate cookie crust

6. **BEAN** a sweet custard pie made with mashed navy beans

7. **DOUBLE CRUST APPLE** best made with tart baking apples that retain their texture

8. **PECAN** filled with a mix of eggs, butter, dark corn syrup or molasses, and whole pecans

June / July 2021

28
MONDAY

29
TUESDAY

30
WEDNESDAY

LAST QUARTER ◑

1
THURSDAY

CANADA DAY (CANADA)

2
FRIDAY

3
SATURDAY

4
SUNDAY

INDEPENDENCE DAY

			JULY			
S	M	T	W	T	F	S
				1	2	3
4	5	6	7	8	9	10
11	12	13	14	15	16	17
18	19	20	21	22	23	24
25	26	27	28	29	30	31

Notes

RED NORTHERN CHITON

PACIFIC PINK SCALLOP

SEASHELLS BY THE SEASHORE

FLORIDA CONE

JUNONIA

SCALY WORM SHELL

CABRIT'S MUREX

CLATHRATE TROPHON

RINGED TOP SHELL

GLOSSY DOVE SHELL

SCOTCH BONNET

ANTILLEAN TUSK

TURBONILLE

HAWK-WING CONCH

ROSE PETAL TELLIN

STRIATE MARGARITE

ATLANTIC YELLOW COWRY

MASK LIMPET

HOOKED MUSSEL

GIANT PACIFIC OYSTER

ATLANTIC JACKKNIFE CLAM

YELLOW COCKLE

DRAGONFLIES

WIDOW SKIMMER

WHITE TAIL

LOW FLYING AMBER WING

DOUBLEDAY'S BLUET

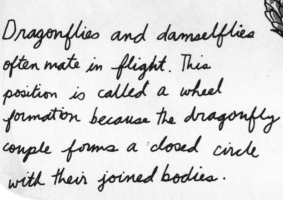

Dragonflies and damselflies often mate in flight. This position is called a wheel formation because the dragonfly couple forms a closed circle with their joined bodies.

5
MONDAY

6
TUESDAY

7
WEDNESDAY

8
THURSDAY

9
FRIDAY

NEW MOON ●

10
SATURDAY

11
SUNDAY

JULY						
S	M	T	W	T	F	S
				1	2	3
4	5	6	7	8	9	10
11	12	13	14	15	16	17
18	19	20	21	22	23	24
25	26	27	28	29	30	31

Notes

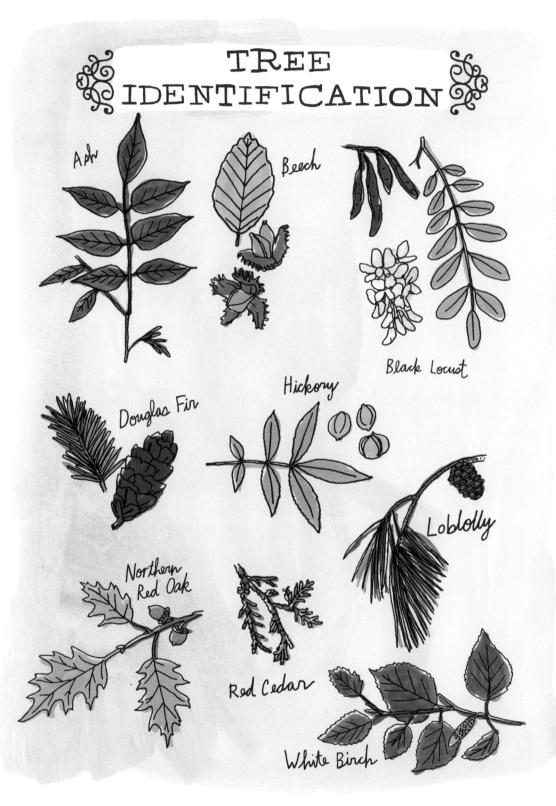

TREE IDENTIFICATION

Ash

Beech

Black Locust

Douglas Fir

Hickory

Loblolly

Northern Red Oak

Red Cedar

White Birch

12
MONDAY

13
TUESDAY

14
WEDNESDAY

15
THURSDAY

16
FRIDAY

FIRST QUARTER ◗

17
SATURDAY

18
SUNDAY

JULY

S	M	T	W	T	F	S
				1	2	3
4	5	6	7	8	9	10
11	12	13	14	15	16	17
18	19	20	21	22	23	24
25	26	27	28	29	30	31

Notes

TURTLES

Turtles' shells are made up of dozens of bones, including outgrowths of the spine and ribs.

SNAPPING TURTLE cannot withdraw completely into its shell

SPINY SOFT TURTLE has a flat, leathery shell and lives buried in mud, with its pointy snout protruding

WOOD TURTLE feeds on mollusks, small animals, and plants

DIAMONDBACK TERRAPIN females sometimes twice the size of males

PAINTED TURTLE social and gregarious, often seen basking on logs together, sometimes on top of each other

19
MONDAY

EID AL-ADHA BEGINS AT SUNDOWN

20
TUESDAY

21
WEDNESDAY

22
THURSDAY

23
FRIDAY

FULL MOON ○

24
SATURDAY

25
SUNDAY

JULY						
S	M	T	W	T	F	S
				1	2	3
4	5	6	7	8	9	10
11	12	13	14	15	16	17
18	19	20	21	22	23	24
25	26	27	28	29	30	31

Notes

SOME WILD-FLOWERS

MOSS PINK
(PHLOX SUBULATA)

SMALL CAMAS
(CAMASSIA QUAMASH)

BABY BLUE EYES
(NEMOPHILA MENZIESII)

CHICORY
(CICHORIUM INTYBUS)

COLUMBIA VIRGIN'S BOWER
(CLEMATIS COLUMBIANA)

FRINGED GENTIAN
(GENTIANOPSIS CRINITA)

26
MONDAY

27
TUESDAY

28
WEDNESDAY

29
THURSDAY

30
FRIDAY

LAST QUARTER ◑

31
SATURDAY

1
SUNDAY

AUGUST

S	M	T	W	T	F	S
	1	2	3	4	5	6	7
8	9	10	11	12	13	14
15	16	17	18	19	20	21
22	23	24	25	26	27	28
29	30	31				

Notes

POPULAR TOMATO VARIETIES

AMISH PASTE

BIG BEEF

COSMONAUT VOLKOV

BRANDYWINE

CELEBRITY

HEALTH KICK

GERMAN

MATT'S WILD CHERRY

TUMBLING TOM

ITALIAN HEIRLOOM

JET STAR

POLISH LINGUISA

SUNGOLD

TIGERELLA

ROSE

2
MONDAY

CIVIC HOLIDAY (CANADA) • SUMMER BANK HOLIDAY (SCOTLAND)

3
TUESDAY

4
WEDNESDAY

5
THURSDAY

6
FRIDAY

7
SATURDAY

NEW MOON ●

8
SUNDAY

AUGUST

S	M	T	W	T	F	S
1	2	3	4	5	6	7
8	9	10	11	12	13	14
15	16	17	18	19	20	21
22	23	24	25	26	27	28
29	30	31				

Notes...

MINERAL NUTRIENTS IN SOIL

Plants extract many essential mineral nutrients from the soil. These are divided into two groups: macronutrients and micronutrients. Primary macronutrients are the major nutrients that plants need the most of for proper growth and survival.

Micronutrients are only needed in tiny amounts. Strange coloration, stunted growth, or multiple buds in plants could be signs that soil is lacking certain nutrients. Doing a soil analysis will determine what those deficiencies are.

Macronutrients

Primary

N NITROGEN **P** PHOSPHORUS **K** POTASSIUM

Secondary

Ca CALCIUM **Mg** MAGNESIUM **S** SULFUR

Micronutrients

 Cl CHLORINE
 Cu COPPER
 Fe IRON
 Mn MANGANESE
 Mo MOLYBDENUM
 Zn ZINC
 B BORON

9
MONDAY   ISLAMIC NEW YEAR BEGINS AT SUNDOWN

10
TUESDAY

11
WEDNESDAY

12
THURSDAY

13
FRIDAY

14
SATURDAY

FIRST QUARTER ◑

15
SUNDAY

AUGUST

S	M	T	W	T	F	S
	1	2	3	4	5	6	7
8	9	10	11	12	13	14
15	16	17	18	19	20	21
22	23	24	25	26	27	28
29	30	31				

Notes

BERRY BASICS

Botanically speaking, all berries are fruits, but not all berries are berries.

Blueberries are true berries — fruits that form from one ovary that are relatively soft and have embedded seeds. (So tomatoes, peppers, and eggplants are technically berries as well.)

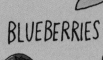

BLUEBERRIES

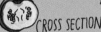

CROSS SECTION

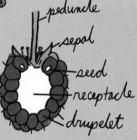

peduncle
sepal
seed
receptacle
drupelet

RASPBERRY

Blackberries and raspberries are aggregate fruits, meaning they merge multiple ovaries.

FLOWER

MULBERRY

Mulberries are multiple fruits: where many flowers grow together.

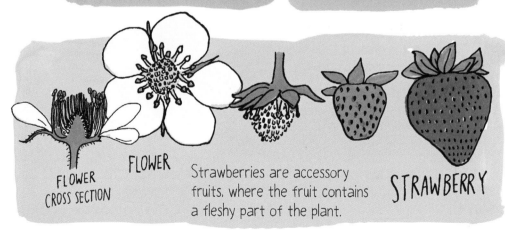

FLOWER
CROSS SECTION

FLOWER

Strawberries are accessory fruits, where the fruit contains a fleshy part of the plant.

STRAWBERRY

16
MONDAY

17
TUESDAY

18
WEDNESDAY

19
THURSDAY

20
FRIDAY

21
SATURDAY

FULL MOON ○

22
SUNDAY

AUGUST

S	M	T	W	T	F	S
1	2	3	4	5	6	7
8	9	10	11	12	13	14
15	16	17	18	19	20	21
22	23	24	25	26	27	28
29	30	31				

Notes

Crop Rotation

To maintain soil fertility and prevent nutrient depletion, farmers rotate the crops they grow each year. Rotating crops also reduces erosion, helps prevent weeds, and controls insect pests.

YEAR 2 — oats

COMMON FIELD ROTATION

YEAR 1 — corn

YEAR 3 — wheat

YEAR 4 & 5 — clover (brings nitrogen back into the soil)

YEAR 2 — onion

COMMON GARDEN ROTATION

YEAR 1 — tomato

YEAR 3

beans (brings nitrogen back into the soil)

YEAR 4 — cabbage

23
MONDAY

24
TUESDAY

25
WEDNESDAY

26
THURSDAY

27
FRIDAY

28
SATURDAY

29
SUNDAY

AUGUST

S	M	T	W	T	F	S
1	2	3	4	5	6	7
8	9	10	11	12	13	14
15	16	17	18	19	20	21
22	23	24	25	26	27	28
29	30	31				

Notes

Common Cakes

ANGEL FOOD CAKE

PINEAPPLE UPSIDE-
DOWN CAKE

CARROT CAKE

BUNDT CAKE

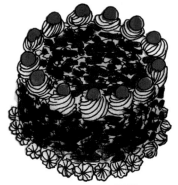

BLACK FOREST CAKE

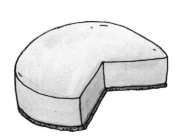

CHEESECAKE

SWISS ROLL
CAKE

MARBLE
POUND CAKE

STRAWBERRY
SHORTCAKE

TORTA TRES LECHES

August / September 2021

30
MONDAY

SUMMER BANK HOLIDAY (ENG., WALES, N. IRE.)

31
TUESDAY

1
WEDNESDAY

2
THURSDAY

3
FRIDAY

4
SATURDAY

5
SUNDAY

SEPTEMBER

S	M	T	W	T	F	S
			1	2	3	4
5	6	7	8	9	10	11
12	13	14	15	16	17	18
19	20	21	22	23	24	25
26	27	28	29	30		

Notes

Horse Terminology

FACIAL MARKINGS

BLAZE · BALD · STAR

SPOT · RACE · STRIPE

LEG MARKINGS

BOOT · SOCK · STOCKING

TAIL STYLES

NATURAL · BANGED · DOCKED · PLAITED

(to keep it out of machinery)

6
MONDAY

LABOR DAY • ROSH HASHANAH BEGINS AT SUNDOWN

NEW MOON ●

7
TUESDAY

8
WEDNESDAY

9
THURSDAY

10
FRIDAY

11
SATURDAY

12
SUNDAY

GRANDPARENTS DAY

SEPTEMBER

S	M	T	W	T	F	S
			1	2	3	4
5	6	7	8	9	10	11
12	13	14	15	16	17	18
19	20	21	22	23	24	25
26	27	28	29	30		

Notes

ANATOMY OF A BUTTERFLY

Canadian Tiger Swallowtail

1. **antenna** - used as a form of radar and pheromone detection
2. **compound eye** - has up to 1,700 individual ommatidia (light receptors and lenses)
3. **palpus** - shields the eye from dust, covered in scent-detecting sensors
4. **proboscis** - like a long straw for feeding and drinking
5. **thorax** - three body segments that contain the flight muscles
6. **forewing** ⎤
7. **hindwing** ⎦ — two pairs of overlapping wings that flap and sometimes glide
8. **wing veins** - vary between each genus of butterfly, used in classification
9. **abdomen** - contains the digestive system, respiratory equipment, heart, and sex organs
10. **legs** - butterflies have three pairs except in the Nymphalidae family
11. **scales** - wings are covered in tiny dust-like colored scales

13
MONDAY

14
TUESDAY

15
WEDNESDAY

YOM KIPPUR BEGINS AT SUNDOWN

16
THURSDAY

17
FRIDAY

18
SATURDAY

19
SUNDAY

SEPTEMBER

S	M	T	W	T	F	S
			1	2	3	4
5	6	7	8	9	10	11
12	13	14	15	16	17	18
19	20	21	22	23	24	25
26	27	28	29	30		

Notes

Umbelliferae / Carrot Family

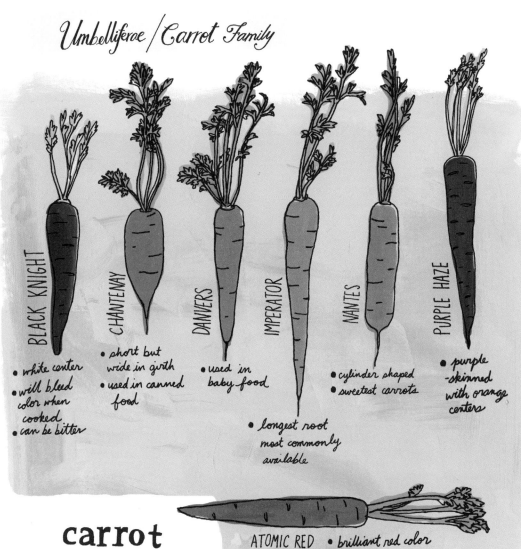

BLACK KNIGHT
- white center
- will bleed color when cooked
- can be bitter

CHANTENAY
- short but wide in girth
- used in canned food

DANVERS
- used in baby food

IMPERATOR
- longest root most commonly available

NANTES
- cylinder shaped
- sweetest carrots

PURPLE HAZE
- purple-skinned with orange centers

ATOMIC RED
- brilliant red color
- high in lycopene

carrot
(DAUCUS CAROTA)

- Carrots are bright orange because of the beta-carotene they contain.
- Eating too many carrots can actually turn your skin orange. The condition is called carotenemia and most often occurs in children and vegetarians.

FULL MOON ○

20
MONDAY

21
TUESDAY

INTERNATIONAL DAY OF PEACE

22
WEDNESDAY

23
THURSDAY

24
FRIDAY

25
SATURDAY

26
SUNDAY

SEPTEMBER

S	M	T	W	T	F	S
			1	2	3	4
5	6	7	8	9	10	11
12	13	14	15	16	17	18
19	20	21	22	23	24	25
26	27	28	29	30		

Notes...

THE FISHMONGER'S LEXICON

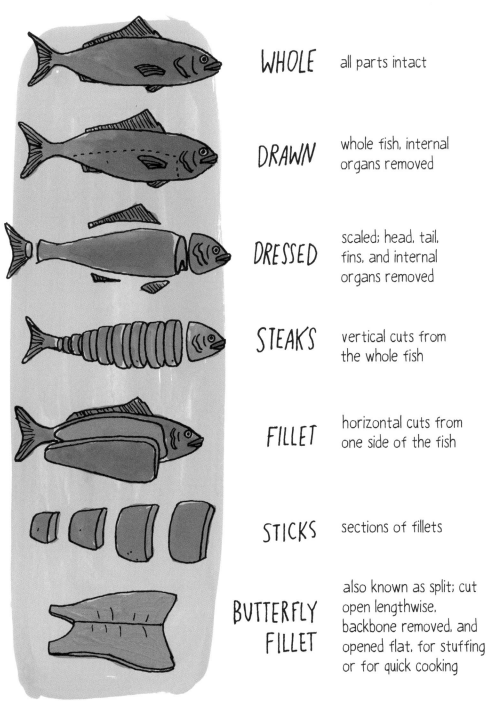

WHOLE — all parts intact

DRAWN — whole fish, internal organs removed

DRESSED — scaled; head, tail, fins, and internal organs removed

STEAKS — vertical cuts from the whole fish

FILLET — horizontal cuts from one side of the fish

STICKS — sections of fillets

BUTTERFLY FILLET — also known as split; cut open lengthwise, backbone removed, and opened flat, for stuffing or for quick cooking

27
MONDAY

QUEEN'S BIRTHDAY (WA AUSTRALIA)

28
TUESDAY

LAST QUARTER ◗

29
WEDNESDAY

30
THURSDAY

1
FRIDAY

2
SATURDAY

3
SUNDAY

OCTOBER

S	M	T	W	T	F	S
					1	2
3	4	5	6	7	8	9
10	11	12	13	14	15	16
17	18	19	20	21	22	23
24	25	26	27	28	29	30
31						

Notes

COMB STYLES

Buttercup

Cushion

Rose

Rose (spiked)

Walnut

Single

Pea

Strawberry

Carnation

V

POPULAR APPLE VARIETIES

AUTUMN
GOLD

BALDWIN

BLACK
TWIG

BRAEBURN

CORTLAND

EMPIRE

FUJI

GALA

GRANNY
SMITH

GOLDRUSH

HARALSON

HONEYCRISP

MACOUN

PINK LADY

RED DELICIOUS

RHODE ISLAND
GREENING

4
MONDAY
LABOUR DAY (ACT, NSW & SA AUSTRALIA) • QUEEN'S BIRTHDAY (QLD AUSTRALIA)

5
TUESDAY

NEW MOON ●

6
WEDNESDAY

7
THURSDAY

8
FRIDAY

9
SATURDAY

10
SUNDAY

OCTOBER

S	M	T	W	T	F	S
					1	2
3	4	5	6	7	8	9
10	11	12	13	14	15	16
17	18	19	20	21	22	23
24	25	26	27	28	29	30
31						

Notes

Tractors Through the Years

Waterloo Gasoline Traction Company built this tractor in 1914. John Deere bought out Waterloo in 1918 and used this popular two-cylinder format for many years.

1914
JOHN DEERE
Waterloo Boy

1948
FORD
8N

In 1945, Henry Ford's 28-year-old grandson, Henry II, took over the company, which was losing money. He created a new tractor with 20 improvements over the previous model. It was a huge success, and over 100,000 were sold in the first year.

In the 1970s, comfort became important. Companies made dust-free cabs with air-conditioning. In this model a filter cleaned the cab air when the doors were shut. A radio, cassette player, and fancier seats were other options.

1973
INTERNATIONAL
1486

October 2021

11 MONDAY
COLUMBUS DAY OBSERVED • INDIGENOUS PEOPLES' DAY • THANKSGIVING (CANADA)

12 TUESDAY
TRADITIONAL COLUMBUS DAY

FIRST QUARTER ◐

13 WEDNESDAY

14 THURSDAY

15 FRIDAY

16 SATURDAY

17 SUNDAY

OCTOBER
S	M	T	W	T	F	S
					1	2
3	4	5	6	7	8	9
10	11	12	13	14	15	16
17	18	19	20	21	22	23
24	25	26	27	28	29	30
31						

Notes

TOAD VS. FROG

Common toad

American green tree frog

TOAD	FROG

- short legs for walking and hopping

- dry, bumpy skin

- stays mostly on land

- no teeth

- non-bulging eyes

- eats insects, slugs, and worms

- long legs for jumping and swimming

- smooth, wet skin

- stays mostly in water

- tiny, sharp cone teeth on the upper jaw

- bulging eyes

- eats insects, snails, worms, and tiny fish

18
MONDAY   MAWLID AN-NABI BEGINS AT SUNDOWN

19
TUESDAY

FULL MOON ○

20
WEDNESDAY

21
THURSDAY

22
FRIDAY

23
SATURDAY

24
SUNDAY

OCTOBER

S	M	T	W	T	F	S
					1	2
3	4	5	6	7	8	9
10	11	12	13	14	15	16
17	18	19	20	21	22	23
24	25	26	27	28	29	30
31						

Notes

❧ WILD CATS ❧

Mountain Lion

More closely related to the domestic cat than the lion, the mountain lion's range extends from northern Canada to southern South America.

Lynx

In the snowy north, a lynx's paw may be larger than a human's hand.

Bobcat

Named for its stubby tail, the bobcat is smaller than its northern lynx cousin and lacks the distinctive ear tufts.

25
MONDAY   LABOUR DAY (NEW ZEALAND)

26
TUESDAY

27
WEDNESDAY

                                                                      LAST QUARTER ◑

28
THURSDAY

29
FRIDAY

30
SATURDAY

31
SUNDAY   HALLOWEEN

OCTOBER						
S	M	T	W	T	F	S
					1	2
3	4	5	6	7	8	9
10	11	12	13	14	15	16
17	18	19	20	21	22	23
24	25	26	27	28	29	30
31						

Notes

ESPRESSO GUIDE

ESPRESSO

RISTRETTO

MACCHIATO

CAFÉ CREME

CAPPUCCINO

AMERICANO

BREVE

MOCHA BREVE

MOCHA

BLACK EYE

CAFFÉ LATTE

CAFFÉ AU LAIT

CAFÉ CON LECHE

1
MONDAY

2
TUESDAY

ELECTION DAY

3
WEDNESDAY

NEW MOON ●

4
THURSDAY

5
FRIDAY

6
SATURDAY

7
SUNDAY

DAYLIGHT SAVING TIME ENDS AT 2:00 A.M. (US & CANADA)

NOVEMBER

S	M	T	W	T	F	S
	1	2	3	4	5	6
7	8	9	10	11	12	13
14	15	16	17	18	19	20
21	22	23	24	25	26	27
28	29	30				

Notes

8
MONDAY

9
TUESDAY

10
WEDNESDAY

FIRST QUARTER ◗

11
THURSDAY

VETERANS DAY • REMEMBRANCE DAY (CANADA)

12
FRIDAY

13
SATURDAY

14
SUNDAY

NOVEMBER

S	M	T	W	T	F	S
	1	2	3	4	5	6
7	8	9	10	11	12	13
14	15	16	17	18	19	20
21	22	23	24	25	26	27
28	29	30				

Notes

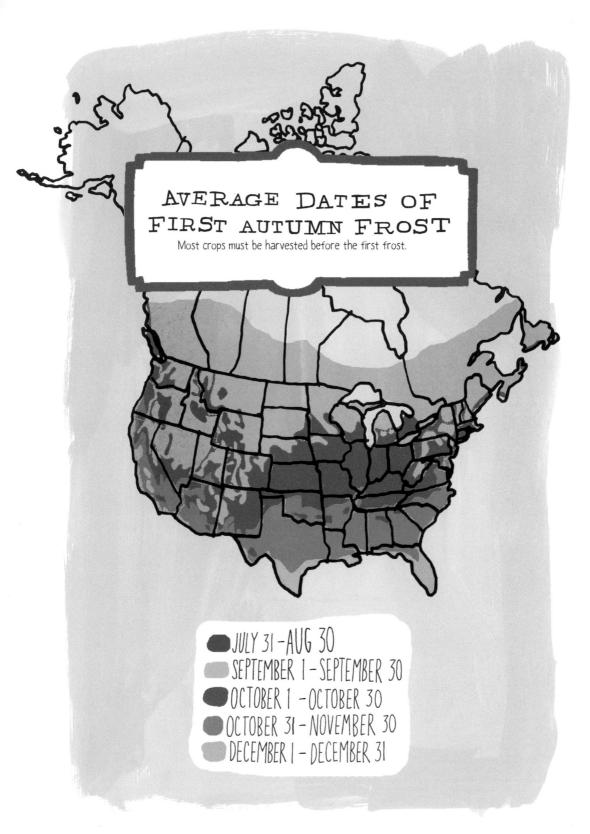

15
MONDAY

16
TUESDAY

17
WEDNESDAY

18
THURSDAY

FULL MOON ○

19
FRIDAY

20
SATURDAY

21
SUNDAY

NOVEMBER

S	M	T	W	T	F	S
	1	2	3	4	5	6
7	8	9	10	11	12	13
14	15	16	17	18	19	20
21	22	23	24	25	26	27
28	29	30				

Notes

A FEW TASTY WORDS TO KNOW

ambrosial. having an exceptionally satisfying taste and/or smell

delectable. exquisitely delicious and delightful, luscious

fetid. smelling awful and unpleasant

gamy. having the flavor or aroma of game, often connotes a slightly spoiled quality

palatable. an okay taste, not particulary amazing but not awful

rich. full-bodied, heavy, robust; often used to describe overly buttery food

sharp. a strong bitter flavor

umami. one of the five basic flavor profiles besides sweet, sour, bitter and salty; a pleasantly round, savory flavor

woodsy. earthy, dirt-like taste, like mushrooms

22
MONDAY

23
TUESDAY

24
WEDNESDAY

25
THURSDAY

THANKSGIVING

26
FRIDAY

LAST QUARTER ◑

27
SATURDAY

28
SUNDAY

HANUKKAH BEGINS AT SUNDOWN

NOVEMBER

S	M	T	W	T	F	S
	1	2	3	4	5	6
7	8	9	10	11	12	13
14	15	16	17	18	19	20
21	22	23	24	25	26	27
28	29	30				

Notes

Tree Shapes

PYRAMIDAL

CONICAL

COLUMNAR

BROAD

VASE

WEEPING

ROUNDED

OPEN

IRREGULAR

29
MONDAY

30
TUESDAY

1
WEDNESDAY

2
THURSDAY

3
FRIDAY

NEW MOON ●

4
SATURDAY

5
SUNDAY

DECEMBER

S	M	T	W	T	F	S
			1	2	3	4
5	6	7	8	9	10	11
12	13	14	15	16	17	18
19	20	21	22	23	24	25
26	27	28	29	30	31	

Notes

REALLY
MOVING

....

northern
hemisphere

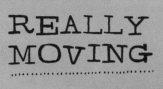

VERNAL
EQUINOX

southern
hemisphere

Spring

The earth spins on its central axis at 1,040 miles per hour, completing one revolution per day. But the earth doesn't stand perfectly upright as it spins. It is always leaning over at about 23.5 degrees.

SUMMER SOLSTICE (longest day of the year)

Summer

Summer is warmer than winter in each hemisphere because the days are longer and the sun's rays hit the earth head-on in the summer and less directly in the winter.

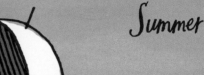

equator

Our planet Earth hurtles through space at nearly 67,000 miles per hour. Its vast oceans and land masses support more than 8 million species of living things, including 7 billion humans.

Winter

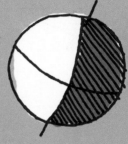

WINTER SOLSTICE
(longest night of the year)

The differences between the four seasons — spring, summer, winter, autumn — are the result of this little tilt in the earth's axis. This tilt causes the hemispheres of the globe to face the sun more directly at different times of the year.

Autumn

direction of orbit

AUTUMNAL EQUINOX

At the equinox, hours of daylight and darkness are roughly equal.

Each year, the earth completes one lap around the sun. Its 585-million-mile orbit is almost perfectly round.

❧OUTSTANDING ADAPTATIONS❧

Short-tailed Shrew

Shrews are among the smallest mammals in the world. This species has venomous saliva for protection and for subduing prey.

Snowshoe Hare

This seasonal chameleon has a stark white winter coat and a brown summer coat. Its name comes from the pads of matted hair on its feet that afford it warmth and mobility on snow.

Porcupine

The porcupine's 30,000 sharp quills are actually modified hairs with barbed tips.

6
MONDAY

7
TUESDAY

8
WEDNESDAY

9
THURSDAY

10
FRIDAY

FIRST QUARTER ◐

11
SATURDAY

12
SUNDAY

DECEMBER

S	M	T	W	T	F	S
			1	2	3	4
5	6	7	8	9	10	11
12	13	14	15	16	17	18
19	20	21	22	23	24	25
26	27	28	29	30	31	

Notes

FERMENTATION

Fermentation is the chemical breakdown and transformation of matter by bacteria and yeasts — it often results in effervescence, heat, and, if we're lucky, sensational foods and drinks. It happens naturally, but by controlling the process and the microorganisms at play, we can also influence flavor.

SWISS CHEESE

WINE

VINEGAR

BEER

YOGURT

SOY SAUCE

PICKLES

KIMCHI

CIDER

MISO

SALAMI

SAUERKRAUT

TEMPEH

SOURDOUGH BREAD

13
MONDAY

14
TUESDAY

15
WEDNESDAY

16
THURSDAY

17
FRIDAY

18
SATURDAY

FULL MOON ○

19
SUNDAY

DECEMBER

S	M	T	W	T	F	S
			1	2	3	4
5	6	7	8	9	10	11
12	13	14	15	16	17	18
19	20	21	22	23	24	25
26	27	28	29	30	31	

Notes

SOME SNOWFLAKE SHAPES

RIMED
CRYSTAL

TRIANGULAR
FORMS

ARROWHEAD

SIMPLE
PRISM

STELLAR
PLATE

STELLAR
DENDRITE

12-SIDED
SNOWFLAKE

FERNLIKE
STELLAR
DENDRITE

20
MONDAY

21
TUESDAY

22
WEDNESDAY

23
THURSDAY

24
FRIDAY

25
SATURDAY

CHRISTMAS

26
SUNDAY

KWANZAA BEGINS • BOXING DAY

DECEMBER

S	M	T	W	T	F	S
			1	2	3	4
5	6	7	8	9	10	11
12	13	14	15	16	17	18
19	20	21	22	23	24	25
26	27	28	29	30	31	

Notes

A VARIETY ❧ OF NESTS ❧

LAUGHING GULL
arranged in beach grass
or found in a shallow hole
in the sand, lined with grasses
and sticks

ROBIN
made of twigs, weeds, grass,
and string, rags and debris,
lined with mud and grasses

YELLOW WARBLER
a cup of stems, wool, and
plant down, lined with fibers,
cotton, and feathers, found
in a forked branch

December 2021 / January 2022

27
MONDAY

28
TUESDAY

29
WEDNESDAY

30
THURSDAY

31
FRIDAY

1
SATURDAY

NEW YEAR'S DAY

NEW MOON ●

2
SUNDAY

DECEMBER

S	M	T	W	T	F	S
			1	2	3	4
5	6	7	8	9	10	11
12	13	14	15	16	17	18
19	20	21	22	23	24	25
26	27	28	29	30	31	

Notes

Basil

Chives

Cilantro

Dill

Marjoram

Mint

Oregano

Rosemary

Parsley

2020

JANUARY

S	M	T	W	T	F	S
			1	2	3	4
5	6	7	8	9	10	11
12	13	14	15	16	17	18
19	20	21	22	23	24	25
26	27	28	29	30	31	

FEBRUARY

S	M	T	W	T	F	S
						1
2	3	4	5	6	7	8
9	10	11	12	13	14	15
16	17	18	19	20	21	22
23	24	25	26	27	28	29

MARCH

S	M	T	W	T	F	S
1	2	3	4	5	6	7
8	9	10	11	12	13	14
15	16	17	18	19	20	21
22	23	24	25	26	27	28
29	30	31				

APRIL

S	M	T	W	T	F	S
			1	2	3	4
5	6	7	8	9	10	11
12	13	14	15	16	17	18
19	20	21	22	23	24	25
26	27	28	29	30		

MAY

S	M	T	W	T	F	S
					1	2
3	4	5	6	7	8	9
10	11	12	13	14	15	16
17	18	19	20	21	22	23
$^{24}/_{31}$	25	26	27	28	29	30

JUNE

S	M	T	W	T	F	S
	1	2	3	4	5	6
7	8	9	10	11	12	13
14	15	16	17	18	19	20
21	22	23	24	25	26	27
28	29	30				

JULY

S	M	T	W	T	F	S
			1	2	3	4
5	6	7	8	9	10	11
12	13	14	15	16	17	18
19	20	21	22	23	24	25
26	27	28	29	30	31	

AUGUST

S	M	T	W	T	F	S
						1
2	3	4	5	6	7	8
9	10	11	12	13	14	15
16	17	18	19	20	21	22
$^{23}/_{30}$	$^{24}/_{31}$	25	26	27	28	29

SEPTEMBER

S	M	T	W	T	F	S
		1	2	3	4	5
6	7	8	9	10	11	12
13	14	15	16	17	18	19
20	21	22	23	24	25	26
27	28	29	30			

OCTOBER

S	M	T	W	T	F	S
				1	2	3
4	5	6	7	8	9	10
11	12	13	14	15	16	17
18	19	20	21	22	23	24
25	26	27	28	29	30	31

NOVEMBER

S	M	T	W	T	F	S
1	2	3	4	5	6	7
8	9	10	11	12	13	14
15	16	17	18	19	20	21
22	23	24	25	26	27	28
29	30					

DECEMBER

S	M	T	W	T	F	S
		1	2	3	4	5
6	7	8	9	10	11	12
13	14	15	16	17	18	19
20	21	22	23	24	25	26
27	28	29	30	31		

Notes

2021

JANUARY

S	M	T	W	T	F	S
					1	2
3	4	5	6	7	8	9
10	11	12	13	14	15	16
17	18	19	20	21	22	23
$^{24}/_{31}$	25	26	27	28	29	30

FEBRUARY

S	M	T	W	T	F	S
	1	2	3	4	5	6
7	8	9	10	11	12	13
14	15	16	17	18	19	20
21	22	23	24	25	26	27
28						

MARCH

S	M	T	W	T	F	S
	1	2	3	4	5	6
7	8	9	10	11	12	13
14	15	16	17	18	19	20
21	22	23	24	25	26	27
28	29	30	31			

APRIL

S	M	T	W	T	F	S
				1	2	3
4	5	6	7	8	9	10
11	12	13	14	15	16	17
18	19	20	21	22	23	24
25	26	27	28	29	30	

MAY

S	M	T	W	T	F	S
						1
2	3	4	5	6	7	8
9	10	11	12	13	14	15
16	17	18	19	20	21	22
$^{23}/_{30}$	$^{24}/_{31}$	25	26	27	28	29

JUNE

S	M	T	W	T	F	S
		1	2	3	4	5
6	7	8	9	10	11	12
13	14	15	16	17	18	19
20	21	22	23	24	25	26
27	28	29	30			

JULY

S	M	T	W	T	F	S
				1	2	3
4	5	6	7	8	9	10
11	12	13	14	15	16	17
18	19	20	21	22	23	24
25	26	27	28	29	30	31

AUGUST

S	M	T	W	T	F	S
1	2	3	4	5	6	7
8	9	10	11	12	13	14
15	16	17	18	19	20	21
22	23	24	25	26	27	28
29	30	31				

SEPTEMBER

S	M	T	W	T	F	S
			1	2	3	4
5	6	7	8	9	10	11
12	13	14	15	16	17	18
19	20	21	22	23	24	25
26	27	28	29	30		

OCTOBER

S	M	T	W	T	F	S
					1	2
3	4	5	6	7	8	9
10	11	12	13	14	15	16
17	18	19	20	21	22	23
$^{24}/_{31}$	25	26	27	28	29	30

NOVEMBER

S	M	T	W	T	F	S
	1	2	3	4	5	6
7	8	9	10	11	12	13
14	15	16	17	18	19	20
21	22	23	24	25	26	27
28	29	30				

DECEMBER

S	M	T	W	T	F	S
			1	2	3	4
5	6	7	8	9	10	11
12	13	14	15	16	17	18
19	20	21	22	23	24	25
26	27	28	29	30	31	

Notes

2022

JANUARY

S	M	T	W	T	F	S
						1
2	3	4	5	6	7	8
9	10	11	12	13	14	15
16	17	18	19	20	21	22
23/30	24/31	25	26	27	28	29

FEBRUARY

S	M	T	W	T	F	S
		1	2	3	4	5
6	7	8	9	10	11	12
13	14	15	16	17	18	19
20	21	22	23	24	25	26
27	28					

MARCH

S	M	T	W	T	F	S
		1	2	3	4	5
6	7	8	9	10	11	12
13	14	15	16	17	18	19
20	21	22	23	24	25	26
27	28	29	30	31		

APRIL

S	M	T	W	T	F	S
					1	2
3	4	5	6	7	8	9
10	11	12	13	14	15	16
17	18	19	20	21	22	23
24	25	26	27	28	29	30

MAY

S	M	T	W	T	F	S
1	2	3	4	5	6	7
8	9	10	11	12	13	14
15	16	17	18	19	20	21
22	23	24	25	26	27	28
29	30	31				

JUNE

S	M	T	W	T	F	S
			1	2	3	4
5	6	7	8	9	10	11
12	13	14	15	16	17	18
19	20	21	22	23	24	25
26	27	28	29	30		

JULY

S	M	T	W	T	F	S
					1	2
3	4	5	6	7	8	9
10	11	12	13	14	15	16
17	18	19	20	21	22	23
24/31	25	26	27	28	29	30

AUGUST

S	M	T	W	T	F	S
	1	2	3	4	5	6
7	8	9	10	11	12	13
14	15	16	17	18	19	20
21	22	23	24	25	26	27
28	29	30	31			

SEPTEMBER

S	M	T	W	T	F	S
				1	2	3
4	5	6	7	8	9	10
11	12	13	14	15	16	17
18	19	20	21	22	23	24
25	26	27	28	29	30	

OCTOBER

S	M	T	W	T	F	S
						1
2	3	4	5	6	7	8
9	10	11	12	13	14	15
16	17	18	19	20	21	22
23/30	24/31	25	26	27	28	29

NOVEMBER

S	M	T	W	T	F	S
		1	2	3	4	5
6	7	8	9	10	11	12
13	14	15	16	17	18	19
20	21	22	23	24	25	26
27	28	29	30			

DECEMBER

S	M	T	W	T	F	S
				1	2	3
4	5	6	7	8	9	10
11	12	13	14	15	16	17
18	19	20	21	22	23	24
25	26	27	28	29	30	31

Notes

Notes

Notes

Notes

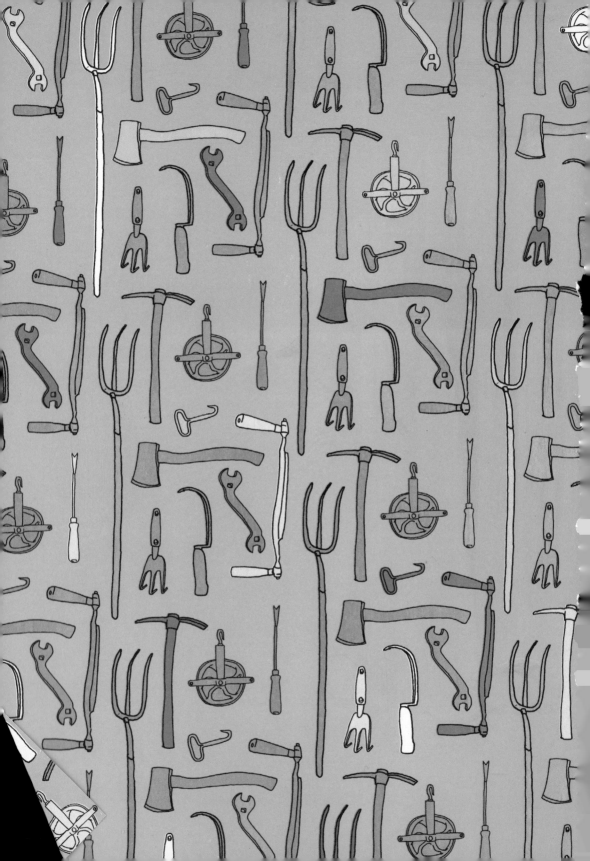